Growing Up

Growing Up

How We Become Alive, Are Born, and Grow

by KARL de SCHWEINITZ

Fourth Edition

The Macmillan Company, New York
Collier-Macmillan Limited, London

PICTURE CREDITS: Black Star, viii (Lambs), 10 (Lockman); Baltimore City Public Schools, 43; National Audubon Society, 8 (Cruickshank), 35 (Le Page); New York Zoological Society, 34, 47; Pennsylvania Fish Commission, 5 (Gordon); Photo Library, 37 (Carmichael), 42; Jack H. Skirball, 28 (from the motion picture The Birth of a Baby, produced for American Committee on Maternal Welfare, Inc.; distributed by Cosmo Films, Inc.); Suzanne Szasz, frontispiece, 20, 21, 36, 46, 49; U.S. Dept. of Agriculture, 33; U.S. Dept. of Health, Education and Welfare—Children's Bureau, x (Bubley), 38 (Bonn), 50; U.S. Dept. of the Interior—Fish and Wildlife Service, 7, 45. Picture research by Patricia Crum. Drawings on pages 12, 16, 24, 26, 29, 30 by Crescent Art Service. Cover photo by Tana Hoban from Rapho-Guillumette.

Preface

Growing Up is for boys and girls who have begun to go to school, both those who can enjoy reading to themselves and those who like to be read to. It is intended for children to whom all or much of the story will be new and for children who want to see in perspective, and review as a whole, what they have already learned bit by bit at different times and in different ways. It is also offered to parents and other adults as a help in answering conversationally the questions which younger girls and boys ask about the reproduction, birth, and growth of human beings and of animals.

In preparing *Growing Up* for its fourth edition, I have drawn upon the personal and professional experience in life and work with children of Elizabeth de Schweinitz, my wife, and have benefited by the advice of specialists in various departments of the Federal Government and in the George Washington University Medical School and Hospital. I have consulted friends who are parents, in particular those who are also engaged in social work, pediatrics, or teaching. I deeply appreciate the help that has come to me from all these interested and understanding persons.

It is significant of the changes which have taken place in attitudes toward sex education that *Growing Up*, which thirty-seven years ago was first published by the Medical and Public Health Department of The Macmillan Company, now appears under the auspices of the Children's Book Department.

KARL DE SCHWEINITZ

Washington, D.C.
March, 1965

Contents

What Growing Up
Is About

Growing Up tells how animals and people become alive, are born, and grow up. People and animals are very much like each other in the way they start living, and much that we have learned about ourselves we have learned by studying animals. Indeed, we are animals too, human animals, but we are also different from all other animals, so different, in such important ways that we call ourselves human beings.

How do human beings and animals start living? How do fish, birds, dogs, horses, rabbits, and lions and people begin their lives? These and other questions I have tried to answer in *Growing Up*.

1
How Animals and People
Start Living

When people and animals are born, they come into the world as babies, human babies and animal babies, but they have not always been babies. Before they can be born, they must first grow to be babies. That means a great deal of growing, for when we begin our lives we are much smaller than we are on the day we are born, and so also are the animals.

When a baby starts growing it is almost too little to be seen. It is smaller than the tiniest dot the sharpest pencil can make. It is almost as round as a ball, and it looks more like an egg than like anything else, and this is exactly what it is—an egg.

All people and all animals begin their lives as

eggs. Dogs, mice, elephants, cats, snakes, birds, worms, fish, even whales, and all other animals start living as eggs, and so do human beings. We come into the world as babies, but before we are born each of us grows to be a baby from an egg.

The little white spot is more than ten times larger than the egg from which you started growing to be a baby.

2
Where Eggs Grow

When we hear the word egg we usually think about chickens. We know that the mother chicken, the hen, lays the egg and that it comes from inside her body. That is where the eggs of all the birds start growing—inside the body of the female. Here also the eggs of fish are formed.

Most fish lay eggs as birds do; but they lay them in streams, in lakes, or in the sea. Some make nests. Other fish drop their eggs in the water, where the eggs float about without any nest to protect them. Fish like salmon, trout, sunfish, shad, and small-mouthed black bass build nests in lakes or rivers and streams. There on the bottom underneath the water they build their nests.

With trout it is the female who makes the nest. With the small-mouthed black bass it is the male who builds the nest. He looks for a place in a river or a lake where there is coarse sand or pebbles or smooth rocks. He pushes his nose into the bottom, as if to make sure that just the right gravel or rock is there. Then he stands in the water with his head pointing up and his tail pointing straight down. He uses his tail like a broom, stirring up the sticks and other rubbish so that the flowing water will carry them away, leaving clean gravel and clean stones. Soon there is a little hollow place in the bottom of the stream. This is the nest.

When it is finished the female small-mouthed black bass lays the eggs. They drop into the nest from a hole on the underside of her body. The eggs are sticky, and they cling to the stones. There are dozens and dozens of them underneath the water. They do not look as if they were in a nest, but that is just where they are. They are in the nest which the father small-mouthed bass has swept clean for them.

After the female has laid the eggs, she goes away. The male stays to guard them, swimming over

Male small-mouthed black bass guarding eggs

them and driving off other fish who might hurt
them.

In each egg there is a tiny part which now starts
growing. We call it the ovum. The rest of the egg—
we call it the yolk—is food for the growing ovum,
which soon doesn't look as if it had ever been part
of an egg. Every day it becomes more and more like
a fish until at last it has changed into a real fish and
is able to swim. How long this growing takes de-
pends very much on the temperature of the water.
If the water is too cold the ovum will grow very

slowly, but if it is just pleasantly cool a little small-mouthed bass will be seen in a few days.

Salmon grow from eggs in the same way that the small-mouthed bass grow, but they take much more time. Some salmon need three months and even longer. Like the small-mouthed bass they make their nests under the water in gravel and where there are clean stones. They choose streams or water along the shores of lakes for their nests, which do not look very much like nests. They will swim for many miles until they find just the right place for their eggs.

With birds it is usually the female who builds the nest, but often the male helps her. Most of the nests we find are in trees or shrubs and bushes. Sometimes we see birds flying into and out of chimneys where they are making their nests. There are also birds which nest in tall grass, which does not seem to be a very safe place. Other birds use little holes in high rocks and still others nest on bare rocks far up on top of steep cliffs.

Inside the body of the mother bird is something that looks like a tiny bunch of grapes, but instead of being grapes the little round balls that hang in

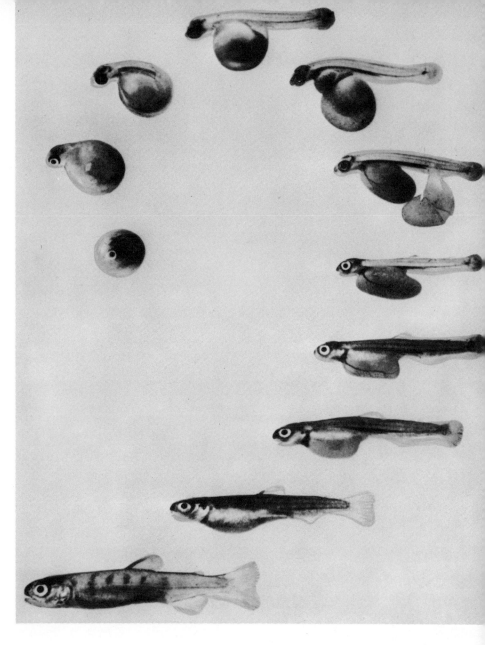

Salmon growing from an egg to a fish

Alder flycatcher on nest keeping eggs warm

a bunch are the ovums, or ova. They are the beginnings of little eggs. The place where the ova grow is the ovary.

The egg stays in the ovary until it is ready to be laid. Then it leaves the other eggs and starts moving through a tube that leads from the ovary to the outside of the body of the bird. The egg has not yet finished growing. Only the yolk, the yellow part, is there, but as the yolk moves along, the white part grows around it. Last of all the shell is added, and now the egg drops into the nest slowly and softly out of an opening under the tail feathers of the mother bird. Then, if she keeps the nest warm by sitting over it, the ovum will start growing to be a little bird. Soon it begins to take up all the room in the eggshell. The little bird will now break the shell and come out into the world.

Some eggs grow to be birds in two weeks; some eggs take longer. Chickens need three weeks to grow from an egg to a chick. While the eggs are in the nest the mother seldom leaves them for a very long time, but some birds do what the ducks do. The duck uses so many downy feathers and other soft things in building the nest that, if she feels like

Chicken eggs hatching in an incubator

flying away for a little while, she can keep the eggs warm by pulling feathers over them. Some mother birds do not leave the nest at all, and the father bird feeds the mother bird. Other birds, like the alder flycatcher, have an even better plan. The father takes turns with the mother in sitting over the nest.

Nowadays most chickens are not raised in nests like those of other birds. As soon as the eggs have been laid, the chicken farmer puts them into an incubator, a row of flat boxes that fit together like drawers in a bureau. Here the eggs are kept as warm as if the hen were sitting on them. Just as with fish, the growing part of the egg, the ovum, feeds on the rest of the egg, which is full of food. The eggs in an incubator are much safer than the eggs of the wild birds, but the farmer must be careful to keep the box in which they have been placed at just the right temperature. If the farmer should forget to do this, no little chicks would come out of the eggs.

But best of all is the way the dog, the cow, the lion, and many other animals take care of their eggs. They do not build nests in the water or high up on rocks or in trees. They keep their eggs in a safer place—in the body of the mother.

The eggs start growing in ovaries like the eggs of the fish and the birds, but when an egg leaves the ovary it does not go into a nest outside the body of the mother. It moves into a nest inside the mother. This nest is like a little bag. It is called the uterus. The egg stays in the uterus until it has grown to be a puppy or a calf or a lion cub or whatever kind of animal the parents happen to be.

Cow with calf in her uterus

This also is the way that we grow to be babies. Inside the body of every woman are two ovaries. They are very small, not much bigger than her thumbs. In one of these ovaries a tiny egg forms. This egg then moves through a little tube into the bag or nest we call the uterus. The uterus is in the middle of the mother's body, below her stomach. There the egg grows to be a baby.

What better place could there be in which to grow? The eggs which fish lay in the water or in nests under the water can be washed away and hurt in storms, and sometimes birds' eggs are broken by being blown out of their nests. But nothing like this can happen to the egg that is growing to be a human baby. It has the best and safest of all nests, the nest we call the uterus, which holds the baby in the middle of its mother's body.

There, in the uterus, the eggs of human beings and the eggs of all animals which start their lives in the bodies of their mothers do their growing. They all grow in very much the same way; and when they are ready to be born they leave their mothers in very much the same way.

3

The Sperm and How
It Finds the Egg

Eggs do not start themselves growing to be fish, birds, animals or babies. Something starts them growing. That something is a tiny creature with a long name. The name is spermatozoon, but usually we call it sperm. It looks a little like a tadpole. It seems to be all head and tail, an almost round little head or body and a very long tail. With the tail it can wriggle and swim. It is many times smaller than the egg, and like the egg it is much too small for us to see except through a microscope.

Sometimes when a fish is split open and cleaned for cooking we find in its body a lot of tiny round balls, thousands of them, all packed together, each about as big as the head of a pin. These are eggs, and the place in which they are packed together is the ovary. We call fish eggs roe and the fish in which we find them is the roe or female fish.

But sometimes we see something that looks like roe but is smoother and softer. It is a kind of jelly. We call it milt. When we find a fish with milt, we know that it is a male fish. In the milt are millions of sperm. The sperm of the male start the eggs of the female growing to be fish.

Fish that have a nest swim over it together, the male close by the female. Then, from a hole near her tail, the female sends the eggs into the water toward the nest. At the same time, the male sends out millions of sperm from a hole near his tail.

As soon as the eggs have left the female and the sperm have left the male, the sperm start swimming toward the eggs. The first sperm to find an egg goes right into it, and together the sperm and the egg start growing to be a fish.

When fish send out the eggs and the sperm we say that they are spawning. Some fish spawn without making nests. The eggs float about in the water and many are not found by the sperm. Even when the eggs are in a nest the sperm may not reach

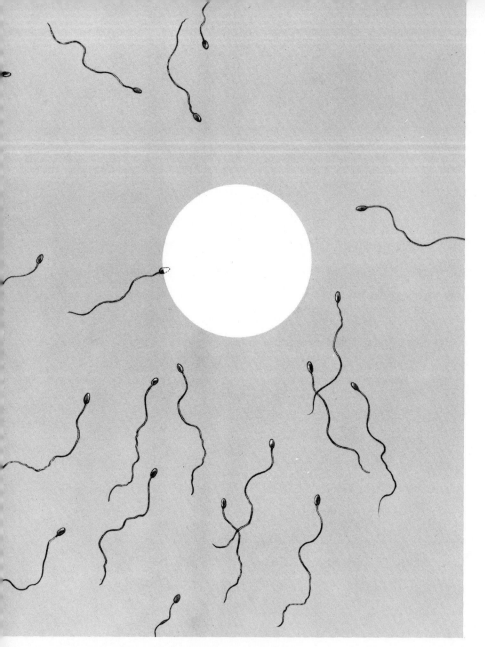

Sperm swimming to an egg

them. A sudden wave may carry the tiny sperm far from the little eggs, and if the sperm do not join the eggs, the sperm die in a very short time.

The sperm of birds are in much less danger of being lost than are the sperm of the bass and the salmon and other fish. The male bird sends them into the body of the mother bird where nothing can harm them and where they can easily find the eggs. On a farm or in any other place where chickens are kept, the rooster can sometimes be seen doing this. He flies onto the back of the hen. When he does this, an opening under his tail feathers meets an opening under the tail feathers of the hen. The sperm can then pass safely from the rooster to the hen.

This is the way in which the sperm of robins, sparrows, catbirds, pigeons, and other birds join the eggs. As soon as the sperm have left the male bird and have gone into the female bird, they find themselves in a tube through which they go toward the egg. Usually they meet the egg just after it has left the ovary. The shell has not yet formed about the egg and one of the sperm goes into the egg. The tail of the sperm drops off, but the head and body of the sperm join the egg. The egg, with the sperm now part of it, starts growing. If after it is laid it is kept warm, it will keep on growing until it has become a little bird, strong enough to break the shell and come out into the nest.

The dog, the lion, the horse, and the cat place sperm in the body of the mother in much the same way that the birds do, but their sperm go through a little tube that is outside the body of the male just in front of and between his hind legs. This little tube is called the penis. When the male sends the sperm to the female he seems to be trying to climb onto her back. As he does this, the penis fits into an opening in her body just above and back of her hind legs. This is the opening of a passage called the vagina, which leads to the uterus of the mother. It is through the vagina that the sperm go when they leave the father.

If you should see a male four-footed animal climbing onto the back of a female animal, or a male bird flying up on the back of a female bird, you might think they are fighting, but they are not. Indeed, the male cannot send the sperm to join the egg unless the female is ready to have him do this.

While the sperm are still living in the male animal they stay in his testes. There are two testes. They are oblong, like very small footballs, and are held in a little bag—the scrotum—outside the body and under the penis. It is also through the penis that the urine or waste water passes, but urine and sperm never leave the penis at the same time.

The sperm of men, like those of the four-footed animals, live in two testes in the scrotum, the little bag under the penis.

The father places the sperm in the body of the mother in much the same way that the four-footed animals do, but more lovingly, and the mother and father can lie together facing each other. The penis, which is usually soft, becomes stiff and then can fit into the vagina of the mother which has its own special opening beneath the opening for the urine or waste water.

When the sperm leave the father they are in something like the milt in which the sperm of fish live. It is called semen. The semen is a little thicker than milk and looks a little like milk. The sperm are so tiny that millions of them can live in one drop of semen.

As soon as the semen has gone into the mother, the sperm start swimming toward the egg. If one of the sperm finds the egg and goes into it, the egg starts growing to be a baby.

This is the way that all people begin their lives. We start living when the sperm joins the egg. This also is the way the animals begin. Fish, birds, cows, lions, dogs, and the other animals start growing in the same way. All of us, people and animals, begin our lives when the sperm joins the egg.

4

From an Egg to a Baby

The egg that has been joined by a sperm is now able to grow, and it starts growing very fast. Its shape changes. At the end of about four weeks the egg of a human being no longer looks like an egg. It seems more like a little curled-up fish. It is still so tiny that it could rest on the nail of the mother's little finger.

It keeps on growing. At the end of eight weeks it is more than an inch long. It begins to look a little bit like a baby.

Even after it has been in the uterus for four months it is still very small, not much bigger than the mother's fist, but it is large enough for the mother to feel it moving. It is lying curled up like

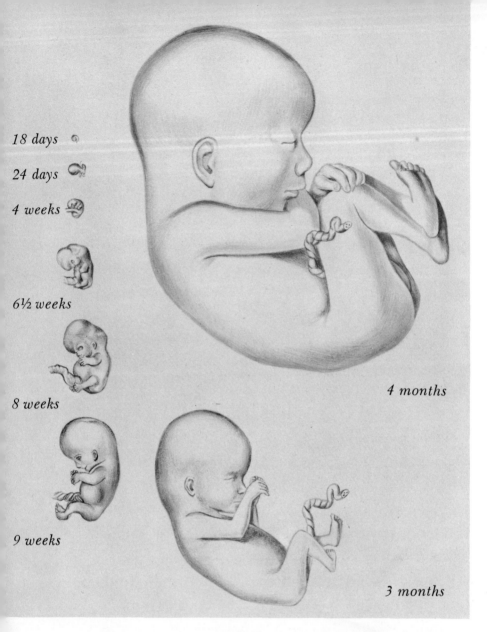

18 days

24 days

4 weeks

6½ weeks

8 weeks

9 weeks

3 months

4 months

From an egg to a fetus of four months. Each drawing is almost the size of the growing baby in the uterus.

a kitten asleep and sometimes it will kick and stretch the way we often do when we are asleep. This tiny living being is called a fetus.

While it has been doing all this growing it has needed food. A long tube comes from its body, ending in something that looks like a flat, round sponge. This is called the placenta. Through the placenta, the baby is fed from the blood of the mother. Every man, woman, and child has a hollow place on the outside of his body that is just below the stomach. People often call it the belly button. Doctors call it the navel. That is the place where the tube goes from the baby to the placenta.

When the egg moves into the uterus and starts growing to be a baby, the uterus is very small, not much bigger than a pear, but as the egg grows the sides of the uterus stretch to make room for it. The mother's body becomes larger. Her breasts grow bigger so that they can fill with milk for the baby to suck from them after its birth.

When the baby has been growing for about nine months, it is ready to be born. The sides of the uterus now stop stretching. Instead they begin to push and to squeeze the baby out. Usually the baby

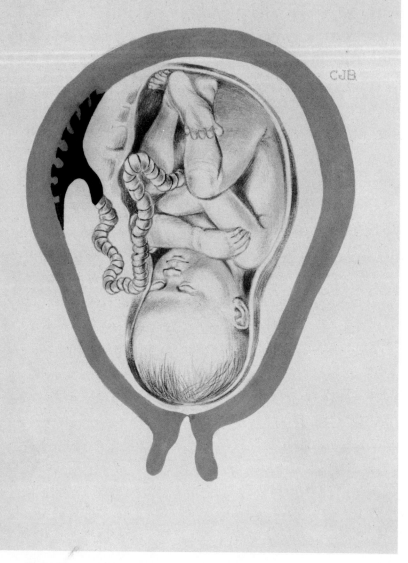

Baby in mother's uterus ready to be born

lies with its head pointing downward toward the tube called the vagina, which leads to the outside of the mother's body. The vagina is narrow, but it stretches as the baby enters it. Slowly the baby passes from the uterus, through the vagina, and into the world. Some babies need a whole day or more in which to make this journey, and some babies are born in a few minutes.

The pushing and stretching that the body must do to help the baby leave the uterus use its mother's strength. It is hard work for her—the doctors call it labor. She either goes to a hospital or calls a doctor to her home. He helps the baby to leave the body of the mother. He cuts the cord or tube through which the food had been going from the mother to the baby, and from now on the baby will feed through its mouth.

The doctor listens eagerly for the first little cry that the baby makes after it is born, for then he knows that it is alive; but the mother and the father are happiest of all, for after having waited so many months, they can at last see the baby and hold it in their arms.

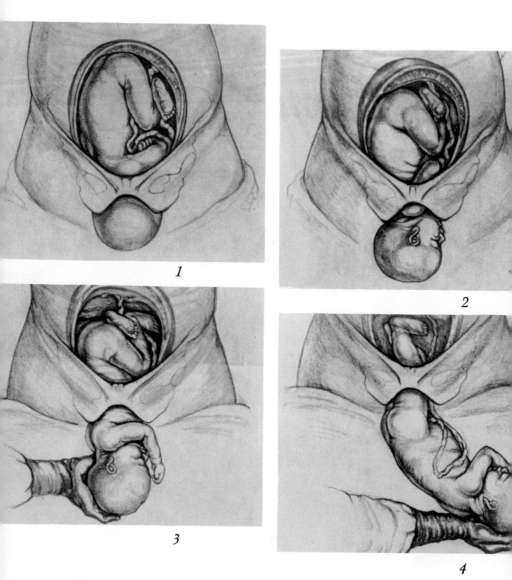

How a baby is born

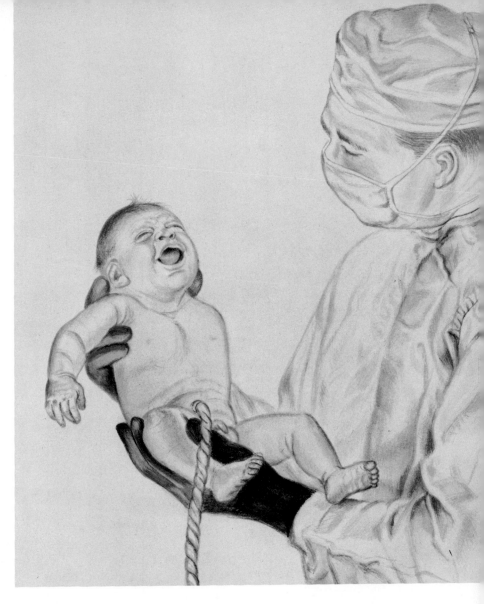

*Doctor holding newborn baby. Its crying helps it breathe.
As the baby no longer needs blood from its mother, the
doctor will cut the cord through which it has been fed.*

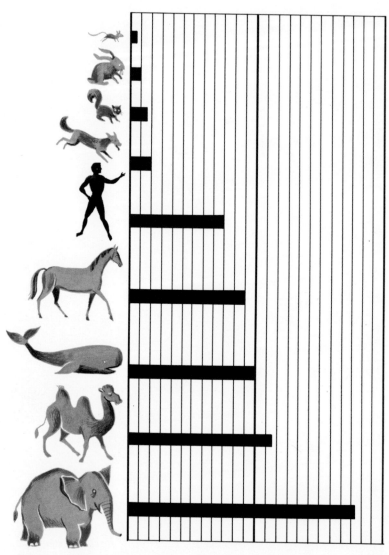

Each space is a month. By counting the spaces you can tell how long each animal takes to become a baby.

5

How People and
Animals Grow

All the animals that grow in the bodies of their
mothers grow in the same way that human beings
grow. The eggs of some animals take much less
time to become babies than do the eggs of people,
and the eggs of other animals take much more time.
A human baby needs about nine months to grow
from an egg but a mouse grows from an egg to a
baby usually in nineteen days. A dog needs about
two months, a horse eleven months, and an elephant over twenty-one months.

But although some animals take more time and
some animals take less time to become babies than
people do, the eggs of animals and of people, when
they start growing, would all look alike to us if we

were able to see them. We would not be able to tell which was the egg of an elephant, an opossum, a mouse, or a human being. A rabbit that has been growing for a week looks very much like a human baby that has been growing for three or four weeks. But the longer the babies of animals and the babies of human beings grow the more different from one another they become.

They all leave the mother's body in the same way. The uterus stops stretching and its sides begin to push the baby out and into the vagina, through which the young animal passes into the world and is born. For some animals, like cows and horses, we now have doctors to help their babies to be born, but most animals take care of themselves and their babies when the time comes for the young to be born.

Usually animals are born in litters, that is, three, four, six, ten, and even fourteen baby animals come into the world one after another from the same mother at the same birth. From three to eight puppies and from three to six kittens are the usual number of puppies or kittens that dogs and cats have, and often as many as fourteen little pigs are

Baby opossums live for a month on their mother's back

born in the same litter. Birds usually have a number of babies; robins have four, sparrows four or five, and chickadees even more.

But most human babies grow one at a time. Sometimes two babies—twins—grow in the body of the mother, and once in a great while there are triplets, that is, three babies at the same birth. There have even been quintuplets, five babies born at one birth. But usually only one baby is born at a time. Some animals, like the elephant, the horse, and the cow, and some birds, have only one baby at a time, but most animals have three or more at a time.

Milk is the first food of human babies and of all animals that grow from eggs in the bodies of their mothers. We call these animals mammals. Mice, elephants, cats, horses, and lions are mammals, and so are men and women. Whales and seals are mammals, for unlike the trout, the bass, the salmon, and most other fish, newborn whales and seals have grown in their mothers' bodies and are fed by their mothers' milk.

Baby deer nursing while mother washes the other fawn

Catbird feeding its babies

Human babies usually take their first milk from the breasts of their mothers. If they are not fed in this way, they are given milk from the cow. Often they drink both their mother's milk and that of the cow. The cow's milk that babies drink comes to us because the calf does not need all the milk the mother cow has for him and because in a very short time the calf stops drinking milk. Like the calf, fish, birds, and other animals eat the same things their mothers and fathers eat long before human babies can eat everything that their parents eat.

Human babies, after they are born, need more time to grow up than animals do. Fish can swim almost as soon as they are hatched. Most birds are ready to leave the nest within two or three weeks after they have come out of the egg. A colt, a calf, or a goat can stand on its feet a few hours after it has left its mother's body.

Most human babies do not walk before they are a year old. Horses, cows, dogs, cats, lions, and most other mammals have usually reached the same

Learning to walk

height as their mothers and fathers by the time they are two years old. Rabbits are full grown in less than a year, and nearly all these animals do not need the care of their mothers for more than a few weeks. In less than two months, a mouse is large enough and strong enough to have babies of its own.

But at two years of age a human baby could not live if its parents did not take care of it all the time. A two-year-old tiger can roam for miles through the forest hunting for food and will not get lost. A two-year-old child would soon be lost if it toddled away from home. Anybody can see the difference between a human child and a grown-up person, but often one must look carefully to tell the difference between a two-year-old horse and one that is much older.

Children have years of growing to do when animals of their age are already grown up. Each year boys and girls are taller and heavier than they were the year before. Somewhere between the time that a boy is twelve and the time that he is sixteen, he usually does his most important growing since he was a baby. His whole body seems suddenly to

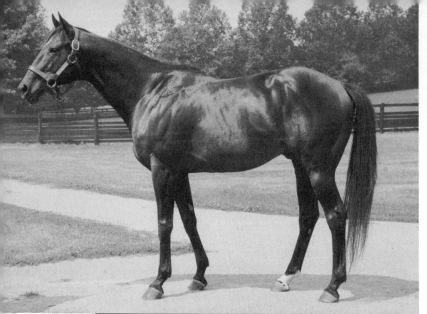

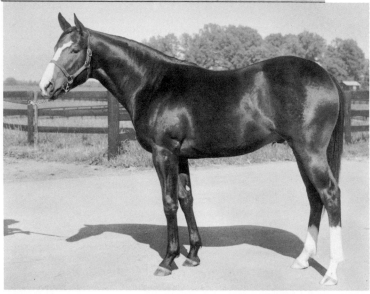

Horse of ten years. One-year-old son. Can you tell the differences between this horse of ten years and his one-year-old son?

become large; his voice becomes deeper; and his strength becomes greater. He then begins to have living sperm in his testes.

Girls do their most important growing usually somewhere between the time that they are eleven and the time that they are sixteen. Their breasts become bigger, and their bodies become larger and stronger. Then about once a month an egg will form in one of the ovaries and will move toward the uterus. The uterus will get ready to receive the egg and will begin growing a new lining just for this purpose. When the egg does not start growing to be a baby the new lining stops growing and leaves the uterus. Then there is a little bleeding. The blood passes out through the vagina. We call this bleeding menstruation. Menstruation usually takes place about once a month after a girl reaches her teens or a year or two earlier.

But if a sperm joins the egg after it leaves the ovary, and the sperm and the egg start growing to be a baby, the lining on the inside of the uterus does not stop growing. It keeps on growing and part of it becomes the spongelike placenta, through which the baby while in the uterus is fed from the

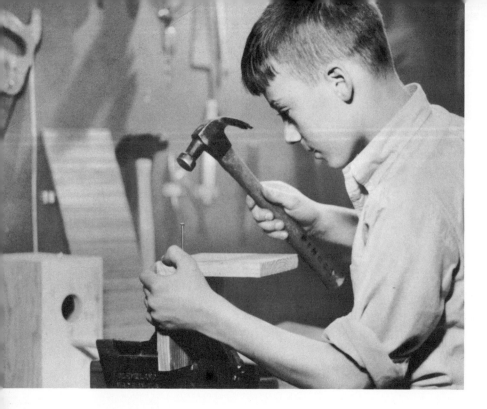

blood of its mother. While the baby is in the uterus menstruation usually stops.

When girls have started menstruating, they are well on the way to becoming women, just as boys are well on the way to becoming men when there are living sperm in their bodies. But both boys and girls have still more growing to do. Sometimes a girl keeps growing in height after she has passed sixteen and a boy may even grow after he is eighteen. People also grow in ways that the four-footed animals do not grow. They learn to think,

42

to read, to write, to use tools, to play games with each other, and to work with other people.

A child grows more slowly than an animal but it learns more than any animal learns. This is one of the great differences between people and all other living creatures. We can keep on growing in mind and in spirit as long as we live.

But when we start our lives, we start as the animals start. We begin growing when the sperm joins the egg, and if we could see the tiny eggs of human babies and of animals when they begin their lives, we would not be able to tell them apart.

6
Marriage and Mating

Spring is the time of the year when most fish spawn and most birds and many animals mate and send the sperm to join the egg. Then their babies can have the whole summer in which to grow before the cold weather comes.

Fall is the best time for the red deer and many other wild animals to start living. They can grow all winter in the bodies of their mothers, and when they are ready to leave the uterus, the spring has arrived and the woods and the meadows are full of food for them to eat.

When fish spawn and animals mate they do not know that they are choosing the best time for their babies to start growing; for, of course, they do not

Salmon leaping upstream to spawn

know that when they send the sperm to join the egg young animals will probably begin living. Fish spawn and birds and mammals mate in the spring or in the fall because the sperm in their testes and the eggs in their ovaries, the way their bodies feel, the sun and the weather, and many other things seem to tell them that the time for the sperm to join the egg has come.

Dogs, cats, cows, sheep, pigs, and the other animals that live with people—we call them domestic animals—mate at various times in the year, not just in the spring or in the fall. Every wild animal and every domestic animal, every bird, every fish, has a time when its body is ready for mating. It is then that the male and the female want to be together. They are more beautiful than at any other time. When the male small-mouthed black bass sees the female bass, his body puts on its brightest colors. He must be very attractive to her as he swims toward and around her, inviting her to go with him over the nest.

When in the spring the birds are ready for mating, the male finds a part of the woods which he takes as his own, and then he begins to sing. His song tells the other males that he now has a spot

Peacock inviting female to be his mate

that belongs to him, and that they are to stay away. The song also tells the female who happens to pass by that here is a male with a place for a nest. She flies toward him.

Then he tries to show her what a fine fellow he is. He may fly high into the air or dart about in all sorts of exciting ways. He may stand on a log or on the ground and dance. At the zoo, one can sometimes see the peacock inviting the female to be his mate. He opens his tail feathers like a fan, blue and green and shining purple. The male turkey spreads his wing feathers until they scrape the ground while he gives his gobble call.

Not many animals wear as bright colors as do the birds, but the male and the female of all kinds of animals have some way of being attractive to each other when the time for mating comes. Then the females of mammals, such as the dog, the cat, the cow, the elephant, have an odor that the males like. Then the antlers, or horns, of the stag have grown to their greatest size, and the call of the cow moose and the answering call of the bull moose can be heard in the forest. Then all the animals have a feeling of life and strength in their bodies. This feeling makes the trout and the salmon swim for miles up the rivers and streams to spawn. It starts the birds singing. It sends the deer roaming through the woods until the male finds the female.

When the time for mating comes the male trout will invite the first female trout he sees to spawn with him; the male bird will usually invite the first female that comes in answer to his singing; and that is what the four-footed animals do. They will usually mate with any other animal of their kind whose body is ready for mating.

Like all other living creatures, men and women want to mate, but they do not mate because the spring or the fall or any other time for mating has come. They marry and mate because they love each other.

When people marry, the man chooses the woman he wants to be the mother of his children, and the woman chooses the man she wants to be the father of her children. They choose the person they love.

It is this love of the father and the mother for each other and for their children that makes the

49

beginning of our lives different from the way in which all other creatures start living. Animals mate because the time for mating has come; people marry and mate because they love each other.

And I can wish nothing better for the boys and girls who read this book than that some day each of you will find someone whom you will love and who will love you and with whom you will have babies of your own. Then you will have lived the whole of the most wonderful of all stories, the story of how we become alive, are born, and grow up.

Index